SUSPENSE AT LAKEFRONT

SUBHAAN

Made with ❤ on the Notion Press Platform
www.notionpress.com

Contents

Foreword

"The Closet Ones Hurt You The Most" - Siddha Smaran
"Trust Is Not Something A Human Can Belittle With " - Ananya

Preface

I wrote this book because I thought of a awesome idea and tried to implement that idea into a book. This book resembles my imagination on text. Although I know I am in 10th and only doing this for some collage credits but still, it works.

Acknowledgements

My friend Siddha Smaran published this book .
There is nothing on this earth more to be prized than true friendship.
Thank You Siddha Smaran ...

Content

CHAPTER ONE

DAY ONE AT LAKEFRONT

"Ugh.... how much longer?" Eva complained.

"We're almost there," Austin replied. It had been weeks since the four of them spent some time together, because of their final tests for college. They knew that they were going to get separated after high school, since Austin was being signed to UCLA for football, Eva got a full-scholarship to Yale for her studies on biomedical science, Tyler was going to stay in Miami and finish his senior year, and Noah had dropped out of high school two years ago.

"M'kay we're here now." Tyler said while parking the car.

"Finally, I'll go get our room while you guys check out the place," proclaimed Noah.

"I'll go with you dude." Tyler sputtered, knowing that Noah would need some help if he went by himself. Once again, Eva and Austin were left by themselves. Not knowing what to say they started unpacking their luggage and headed out to the reception desk.

"Nice place huh," Austin mentioned while looking in Eva's eyes.

"Yeah it's awesome, look it's Noah and Tyler let's go!" Eva exclaimed.

"Did you get the keys guys?"

"Nah, apparently someone booked or room at another location." Tyler said while glaring at Noah.

"I thought that you booked it Tyler." Austin continued

"Guys it's fine let's just go to, where are we going?" Eva questioned.

"Uhm to LakeFront.." Noah said in a disappointed voice.

"Wait no way, you're kidding right, that's like the second worst resort in Miami." Austin pleaded

"It's probably not that bad, c'mon guys it's only half an hour away." Eva replied.

Eventually, all of them reach LakeFront and their expectations were blown away. The rooms were highly advanced and were half the price. Eva quickly gave the money and took the key to the room. She opened the door to see a modern and fully furnished room and falls on the bed. Surprised by the rating 2.56 of LakeFront, they decided to check out the reviews for the place.

"Highly unprofessional, and dust almost everywhere, even on our towels! Oh here's another one, they didn't even provide a coffee machine or bottles of water, there was crust everywhere on the walls." Noah read from his phone with a concerned look

"Huh, there isn't any of those problems here, must've been written by some Karen's," Tyler chuckled.

"Or they updated the place because of those comments," Austin replied in a serious tone while resting on his mattress. "Anyways lets go check the place out," Austin said while the others followed him out the door. The resort's features were more extensive and ravishing then they thought it would be. They saw several waterslides near the lake, with jet skis, canoes, and boats near the docks on the westside of the resort. The food court had more variety than they could've wished for, from; Chinese, Mexican, Hawaiian, Italian, French, Indian food and many more cuisines. But the only thing everyone wanted was to sit in the surprisingly large hot tub near the swimming pool.

"Lets go get changed and go to the hot tub guys,"

Noah exclaimed, running to the elevators. They reached the hotel room and started to get changed taking turns while taking turns in the bathroom. Eva walked out the bathroom with her bikini on, ready to go on downstairs.

"You look great Eva," Austin murmured as the words fell from his mouth.

"Uhm thanks," She replied back not knowing he was still staring at her

"She's so beautiful, I shouldn't have left her," Austin thought.

It had been six months since Austin and Eva broke up. However, Austin still couldn't get over the fact Eva had moved on first. He couldn't help seeing both of them as just friends now that they're over. It didn't matter much anyway, after summer break they were both going to go their separate ways, so he couldn't think about her too much once college started.

CHAPTER TWO

THE RESTAURANT

"You guys go ahead I'll catch up," Austin remarked to the others after he changed in to his swim trunks.

"Okay we'll see you down there!" Noah exclaimed while panting down the hallway. Turning the keys with a sigh, Austin headed towards the glass elevators.

"Ring, ring!" Austin's phone rang. It was the director of sports for UCLA, the man who gave Austin his football scholarship, the one thing Austin was actually proud of. However, Austin hanged up and looked down at the clear glass floor of the elevator as it descended to the ground floor. The man called again, hoping for a response, but Austin refused yet again to answer his phone.

He reached the bottom of the ground floor and walked towards the swimming pool area, while the other teenage girls looked at him in awe.

"Looks like your getting all the ladies tonight," Tyler laughed.

"Don't worry I'll save some for you guys," Austin fake chuckled, to set the mood. It was just the four of them in the hot tub, while Noah and Tyler started debating on whether Cristiano Ronaldo or Lionel Messi is the better football player.

"So how's Chloe doing?" Austin asked Eva.

"She's great, we went to the movies the other night," Eva replied.

"That's cool, yeah th-that's great," Austin stuttered back.

"Excuse me sir?" a woman in a uniform said while handing out a flyer.

"Yes?" Austin replied, taking the flyer from the lady.

"We're having a private event for resort residents at our newly opened restaurant, Brownstone Bistro." the woman told Austin.

"Cool, thank you we'll check it out soon." Austin murmured. "Do you guys want to check out this today?"

"Yeah, lets do it." Noah answered back. After an hour in the hot tub they all headed back to their room, to get changed in their formal wear.

"Guys I didn't bring any jeans, Noah do you have some?" Austin asked as Noah threw some jeans in his face. Eva pulled a tiny plastic bag from the back of her suitcase pocket, and slipped in the back of her handbag while Austin watched her. They locked the room and headed up stairs to Brownstone Bistro.

As they reached the restaurant, the reception man looked extremely familiar to Austin.

"Good evening, and welcome to Brownstone Bistro foll-" the man said while taking a closer look at Austin.

"Austin Kline, is that you?" the man questioned while staring at

Austin.

"Yes, are you Coach Bentley?" Austin replied.

"Man, its been so long, your so much older now, how's football going?" Coach Bentley asked

"It's been really good so far, I got in to UCLA." Austin replied while looking at Noah's impatient face. "You guys go ahead, we'll just catch up and I'll join you soon." Austin said smiling. Eva, Tyler, and Noah had a seat at and the waiter handed out water to all of them including Austin.

"Oh dang it, I forgot my phone, Eva can I have the keys?" asked Tyler while Eva handed him the keys.

"Ring, ring!" Noah's phone rang, it was his girlfriend, Alissa, who had started dating Noah since his family was very wealthy (gold digger bitch). Noah answered the call and started walking around, not noticing what Eva was doing.

Eventually, Tyler came back panting with his cell phone and Austin sat down while Noah was saying bye to his girlfriend.

"No you say bye first, no, no you say it first." Noah babbled over and over again.

"Noah we don't have all day, c'mon get of the phone." Tyler scolded. Noah finally walked back to his seat next to Austin. Looking at Eva in her beautiful turquoise short dress, with her curled hair, made Austin ashamed as he was wearing a plaid shirt and a pair of jeans

"Uh, I have to go to the bathroom," says Austin

"Yeah, me too," Tyler exclaimed. The both of them left to the bathroom, but only Tyler came back.

CHAPTER THREE

THE BATHROOM STALL

"Can we get something to eat in the meantime?" Noah pouted impatiently.

"Okay I guess," Eva replied, as she raised her hand for the waitress to come to our table.

"I'll get sushi, no soup, no pizza,... yeah I'll get pizza," I said looking at the variety of foods on the menu, but the one thing I wanted wasn't on the menu, tortilla chips and guacamole.

"Too bad they don't have any Mexican food here, huh Tyler?" Noah chuckled while looking at me.

"I'll take the steak, uhm medium rare, also I only eat steak that's been cooked on a grill with just a bit of salt." Noah said, while all his impatience had suddenly disappeared off his face.

"Yup, that's how steak is made sir," the waitress said with a heavy sigh.

"Do you want to order for Austin too?" I asked Eva as she searched through her bag, looking for something important. She ordered herself a bowl of broccoli cheddar soup and ordered Austin his favorite, spaghetti with meatballs. We all knew what happened once Austin and Eva broke up, they were so perfect, but Austin wanted football more. I'm not sure he's happy with his decision ever since Eva and Chloe started dating.

It had been almost a half an hour since Austin had been in the bathroom, so Noah went to go and check on him. After a few extremely long minutes, Noah came back saying that he probably isn't done in the bathroom.

"I wonder what he ate" I laughed while Noah took his seat. We had got our food including Austin's, but we were still wondering whether or not we should start without him. Noah, being eager to eat his steak, started without us.

"I'll go check up on Austin, and come back." As I walked to the bathroom stall, I could see a tiny plastic bag opened and left on the tile of the ground. I saw Austin's foot sticking out of one stall and started knocking on the door.

"Austin, we got our food, are you done yet?" I asked in a calm voice. He didn't respond.

"Austin, are you done going to the bathroom yet? Our food is here." I said in a louder voice, still no response.

"Hello Austin? Mom said you have to quit football." I told him, trying to evoke him to come outside.

"Austin, Austin, hello c'mon man open the door!" I hollered hoping he would respond this time, but he didn't. I started banging the stall door, in hope that I would open it. Out of no where, I started to cry, I knew something wasn't right, Austin always answers even if he is mad. After a few minutes, two waiters came and asked me what the problem was, I told them about Austin, and they grabbed some tools from the back of the restaurant to open the door.

"Tyler, is everything alright? What's wrong, why are you crying?" Noah asked me franticly. I walked out of the bathroom and told Eva and Noah what had happened. Before they could say anything, the two waiters urged all of us to come in to the bathroom immediately. They had managed to remove the door of the stall Austin was in.

I couldn't believe my eyes. With one foot stretched to its full capacity, the other bent to the side, his head sagged up towards the ceiling, while white powder covered his shirt and the top of his lip.

Austin was dead.

CHAPTER FOUR

DEATH

Tyler had a dreadful look on his face while the waiter's were still trying to comprehend what had happened. One of the waiter's called the police and informed them about what happened to Austin.

"Ha-how could this happen," stuttered Tyler. He looked in to our eyes, filled with tears and gave us a tight grasp.

The police arrived and took samples of the white powder to investigate it. Eva looked at the tiny plastic bag that one of the inspectors picked up and fell to her knees in tears. As if she was the one who caused this.

Eventually, Austin's parents along with the ambulance arrived and took Austin on a stretcher to the hospital. They told us to wait in the lobby of the restaurant, while they called the police department, and made final decisions. I looked at Tyler's face which was completely red, from crying so much. Whereas Eva's mascara ran down her face as she was crying too.

The police officers along with a few investigators came out of the bathroom while taking all their evidence.

"Lets go," the officer said in a dull, piercing tone.

"Okay, thank you officer," I said while all of us stood up to leave. All of a sudden I felt a tight pull on both my arms.

"You three are coming with us," an officer scolded. We all got hand cuffed and were pushed out the door.

"You don't understand, we didn't do anything, we're innocent!" I started hollering so at least one of the officers would understand me. After much convincing from myself and Tyler, we were all thrown in the back of a police car. What were my parents going to think? They can't bare to think their only son would be put in jail.

This wouldn't be happening. This wouldn't be happening if I had never met Tyler, Eva or Austin. This wouldn't be happening if Austin thought twice about what he was doing. Or did someone do this to him? Maybe that's why the police were taking us, to investigate who did this to Austin. However, Austin wouldn't have done this too himself, he had everything he wanted, everything he needed, apart from Eva.

But it couldn't have been one of us who did it. We all loved Austin, he was like a brother to all of us. Why were they taking us without any proper evidence? They don't know if one of the waiters put some cocaine in to his water, or if Austin ate something before coming to the restaurant. Although, I knew all of us wanted to figure out why and how this happened to him.

After a extensive 30 minute drive, we finally reached the police station and they dragged us to the back of the station. Being quite wealthy, I had never been treated like this before. This treatment enraged me, but I know we were doing it for Austin, so I kept my mouth shut.

Next thing I know, each of us are throw in different rooms. For investigation.

CHAPTER FIVE

INTENTIONS

"Get your hands off me!" I heard Tyler holler from the room across from us.

The fact that my 2 best friends and I were getting interrogated finally hit me like a blast of cold wind to my stomach. They sat me down in a hollow, dark, dead room, like the ones in the movies. As they throw me upon a chair, I try to steady myself, however I can just feel my heart aching of pain. My head starts to get dizzy, I feel my hands and face start to sweat, and I can't stop my legs from shaking.

They start asking me questions.

"Please state your name and date of birth please," one police officer asked in a stone cold voice.

"M-my name is Eva Cabot, I was born on the 15th of June in 2003." I answered in a worried, soft voice.

"Good, now state your relation with Austin Kline." the same officer said.

Suddenly everything hits me, it's like I'm frozen in time. It's like I didn't notice a thing. Austin Kline. Not just my ex-boyfriend, but my bestfriend, my first friend. How did this happen? Who did this too him? And why? The different scenarios of what could've happened suddenly came to my mind. The last time I saw Austin was when he went to the bathroom with Tyler, but it couldn't have been him, right?

I remember the tension between us at the hot tub, while Noah and Tyler were talking. I could see him playing with his ear, he does that when he's nervous. I didn't even try to make him feel better, instead I just talked about Chloe. I know Austin had completely shattered once I told him about Chloe and I, I didn't intend for him to get hurt like he did. Those weren't my intentions, I just wanted to escape. Escape from the pain I felt of Austin leaving me to pursue his career.

"Hello, Eva? Can you please answer my question?" the police officer said, as he interrupted my thoughts.

"Oh, uhm yes. Austin was my best friend, and also my ex-boyfriend." I say as the police officer looks at me skeptically.

"Who did you see last with Austin?" the police officer queried, while staring at me.

"Tyler." I whispered as the word fell out of my mouth. The guilt hit me the instant I said his name. I can't believe I had blamed Austin's own brother

"Are you sure?" the officer argued for conformation. I could feel the hand cuffs start to clench my hands tighter and tighter. My throat started to get dry, my chest pounding at what felt like a mile per second. I can't believe he was questioning me, I already gave him my answer.

"Yes. I'm sure." I answered back in a serious yet clear voice. The officer looked at me in a dead tone, as if he was looking through my eyes. I know I shouldn't have blamed Tyler, but I did suspect him. They told me to stay in town, and just like that I was dismissed from the room.

CHAPTER SIX

MEMORIES

"State you name and date of birth," a middle aged police officer instructed me.

"My name is Tyler Hill Kline, I was born on the 18 of December, 2004." I answered in a shaky voice. He looked at me in concerning way, as if I had anything to do with Austin's death. He looked at his journal and turned pages back and forth as if he was in a rush.

"So it seems you were the last person that was with Austin before his death," he croaked with a pause. "Is this true?" he finished. I looked back at the events before the incident, I realized all the evidence pointed to me. I was the last one with Austin and the first one to find him dead. Although, I wanted to believe this was all a coincidence, I know someone had made all the evidence point to me. The question was, who?

"As it seems, yes, yes I was." I muttered back to the police officer, with my head facing down, trying to find all the facts. It couldn't have been Noah or Eva, right? But they were the only ones with Austin, besides me. Maybe it was Coach Bentley, but he wouldn't have known Austin was coming to the restaurant in the first place.

I still remember when Austin found me in the alley way between 4th street and Park Avenue. He asked who I was and why I was there, so I told him my story. My birth mother told me we were playing hide and seek, so I hid in that exact alley next to the gray trashcans which matched my shirt at the time. However, she never found me, and I never found her, I was only 9 years old. Austin took me to his house while he was heading back from football practice, he was just 11 years old then, yet so selfless.

The tears started rolling down my face like cold rain in the dark streets. The officers gave me extra time before they asked me the next question, as they could see I was crying. I looked up at the officer while nodding, signaling that I was ready for the next query.

"Do you suspect anyone?" The officer glanced at me in a heavy voice. I remembered Eva sneaking a white packet in her hand bag before we went to the restaurant, however I'm not completely sure if it was her cocaine. But it was all over Austin's shirt, some sort of white powder smeared on his cheek and shirt.

"Eva." I answered in a boldly.

"Eva Cabot?" The officer queried.

"Yes, Eva Cabot." I clarified. They sent me out of the room, and told me not to leave the town, otherwise they will find me. I was told to stay at home for 24 hours, in case of an emergency. I was the first person dismissed from the station, as I heard the voices of Eva and Tyler still in the rooms. I heard my name coming from the investigation room Eva went into, I heard her voice muttering my name. Did she suspect me? Or was she defending me? I trembled down the narrow walk-way of the police station, and opened the door of the exit.

I sat in my car with a heavy sigh, and headed back home with over whelming stress. While a phone rang in the backseat.

CHAPTER SEVEN

CONFUSION

"Let go of me!" I hollered at the police officers. They threw me against the glimmering metal chair.

"Do you know who my father is?" I yelled questioningly as they stared through my soul. One of the police officers sat down in an identical chair as mine with a slight smirk around the right side of their face. While the other officer stood up with a dark, cold look on his face. I could feel my back clenching with unbearable pain as they hand cuffed me.

"I shouldn't have worn a jacket." I thought as the sweat started pouring from my face.

"Nervous aren't you?" the officer said as he slammed his hand on the table with a large grin on his face. This was a basic 'good cop, bad cop' situation. The officer in the chair was obviously the good cop, whereas the one standing up seemed absolutely ruthless. I gulped while looking in to the officers eyes. I could feel myself shaking, but I still kept a tough appearance on the outside. Looking up, the officer asked me a question.

"Please state your name, your date of birth and your relationship with Austin Kline." the officer in the chair announced. I looked down to the gritty floor of the hollow room. I don't know Austin as well as Eva and Tyler do, however we both wanted the best for each other. Everything was going well for him, he was signed to one of the best colleges in the country. I first met Austin when Tyler introduced me to him in the 10th grade.

We didn't like each other as much as we did then, although our friendship grew over time. He knew more about me more than I know about myself.

"Answer the question, son!" the rude police officer said abruptly with a stomp to the ground.

"Ok." I talked back. "My name is Noah Jackson, I was born on the 5 of September of 2004. I was Austin's friend who I was introduced to by his brother, Tyler about 2 years ago." I replied, looking deeply in to the officer eyes.

"Alrighty good, now who do you suspect?" The officer enquired. I was lost, I didn't have any evidence for who it could be. Its like my memory had washed away, the only thing I could remember was the sight of finding Austin in the stall. I told the officer I didn't have a suspect as I couldn't find any proof. The officer in the chair asked me a few more questions before I left the room. I could tell Tyler was finished with his investigation, as his door was left wide open. However, I could still see Eva's silhouette through the gray blurry glass as I headed out the door.

CHAPTER EIGHT

PICK UP

I walk to my car with a heavy sigh after exiting the police station. I start the car back to the hotel. The hotel is surprisingly only 5.6 miles from where I live, making it easier to drive home to deliver the news about today. I turn in to the parking lot to pick up my luggage from the hotel, while a few police officers were still at the hotel trying to calm the situation down.

"You're name, and reason of entering ma'am?" one of the officers enquired me before i went through the hotel doors.

"My name is Eva, and I'm here to get my stuff out of my room." I replied back while looking at the people around the counter.

"Were you at the crime scene miss?" the officer said while I noticed that he was one of the officers which entered Tyler's investigation room.

"Yes sir, I was, they took my to the station where I finished answering my set of questions." I answered sternly to the police officer. He stood there for a moment staring into my eyes, as if he was trying to confirm if I was telling the truth.

"Alrighty, go ahead ma'am." the officer said as he made an entering gesture. I walked inside the hotel lounge to the elevators, while most of the staff looked at me as if they've seen a ghost. As I reached our hotel room I could see a group of 5 officers inspecting our room.

"Excuse me?" I asked tirelessly while the insides of our luggage were being thrown apart.

"May I get my stuff please?" I questioned to one of the police officers who looked at me.

"Ma'am, this is your room?" the officer doubted me.

"Yes sir, it is." I replied while trying to find a way inside. The cop stopped me. He made sure I was in my original position before he started talking.

"We are investigating your bags and belongings, due to the situation we won't be able to let you collect them, unless we call you back to the station after the investigation." the officer explained in a thorough manner. I looked back and forth at him and my luggage in a concerned way. He nodded his head and consoled me to head home while patting my back.

I walked out the lobby of the hotel and headed back home, hoping that they wouldn't find my secret.